The Antler Woman Responds

The Antler Woman Responds

By
Ki E. Russell

Paladin Contemporaries * Scottsdale * Kansas City, Missouri

Copyright ©2014 by Ki E. Russell.

All rights reserved. Printed in the United States of America.

First Edition. Except for brief quotations embodied in critical articles and reviews in newspapers, magazines, radio or television, no part of this book may be reproduced by any means electronic, mechanical, or placed in any information and retrieval system without written permission from the publisher.

For information and permission, contact

Paladin Contemporaries
6117 E. Nisbet Road
Scottsdale, AZ 85254

Library of Congress Cataloging-in-Publication Data

Russell, Ki E.
The Antler Woman Responds: poetry /First edition.

ISBN-13 978-1-881048-07-7
ISBN 1-881048-07-1
    1.   Poetry. 2. Mythology. 3. Fairy Tales.

"Antler Woman." Cover art by Ki Russell.

Paladin Contemporaries, Scottsdale, Arizona. Kansas City, Missouri.

For Veronica, in all of her faces.

Acknowledgments

"Drowning in Pearls," "Infatuectomy," "In the Dark" *Electric Velocipede* Fall 2010.

"Adam's Revenge" *Bare Root Review*, Fall 2007.

"Every Night is a Night of Bombs Somewhere" *Splinter Generation*, 2012.

"Thoughts While Smoking the Last Cigarette on the Porch in Summer" *Rio Grande Review* Fall 2009.

"The Antlered Woman Responds" *Sugar House Review* Fall 2009 / reprinted *Moment of Change.*

"Labyrinth" *Kaleidotrope* October 2010.

"Evening Bread" *Etchings* #8.

"Midnight Scenes" *Midwest Quarterly* October 2013.

Contents

Annunciation

"The Gospel According to the Antler Woman," 3
"Drowning in Pearls," 5
"Adam's Revenge," 7
"Every Night is a Night of Bombs Somewhere," 9
"Thoughts while Smoking the Last Cigarette on the Porch in Summer," 10
"Tell Stories if You Want the Adults to Listen," 11
"The Antler Woman Responds," 12
"A Warning, Maybe," 13
"Margaritas, Poolside," 14
"Half Light," 15
"Frying Green Tomatoes," 16
"Infatuectomy," 18
"In the Dark," 19
"Midnight Scene," 20
"Why I Smoke in the Morning," 21
"Reading Fitzgerald in June," 22
"In *el Mercado*," 23
"Dear Prufrock," 24
"First Communion," 25
"Cutting the Cake," 28
"In the Studio, After," 29
"No Bukowski," 31
"Nataraja on Broadway," 32
"Hitchhikers," 33
"My Daughter's Monologue," 34

Healing

"After Encephalitis," 37
"Eric, after the Throat Slashing," 39
"Faulkner's Rebellious Woman," 41
"Seasonal Sleep," 42
"Rainy Supper," 43
"A Dozen Small Perceptions before Dusk," 44
"Labyrinth," 46
"Breakfast, Too Early, on the Patio in June," 48
"Evening Bread," 49
"Massaged by Hooves," 50
"Gaea's Saturday Morning," 51
"Ingesting the Storm," 52
"Baby Book," 53
"Business Lunch," 54

Revelation

"Industrial Revelation," 57
"Treading Water with Uncle Bill," 58
"Urban Primitive," 60
"Swamp Swim," 62
"Bath," 63
"Lactation Lament," 64
"Dead Mermaid," 65
"Shake the Dust from My Tongue," 66
"A Defeated Caffeine Junky Remembers the War," 67
"Scout," 68
"Insomnia Rag, Minor Key," 69
"Discussing the Romantics," 70
"Storyless," 71
"Buddy at the Casino," 72
"A Retired Miner Describes Work," 73
"Bedroom Mutation," 74

Annunciation

The Gospel According to the Antler Woman
In the beginning was the Word, and the Word was with God, and the Word was God. (John 1:1)

I

Curve your tongue
under syllables.
Let phoneme crash
phoneme. Move
among morphemes.
Speak to the wind.
Call particles out of air.

II

Let the core beat
of the whirling
terrain ricochet
through your vapor.
Listen to soil-smeared
words twine around
 hooves and sprout
from skulls. Sharpen
your horns on syllables.
Open your eyes to that dark.

III

Now breathe a name
for the universe.
Chisel the name
in rock and carve
existence. Pen a planet's
path. Write until worlds
twirl through space.
Speak from your skin.

Drowning in Pearls

A strand of pearls bumps up my throat and the orbs drop
one by one from my lips. The last pearl catches in my teeth

and I unhook the strand. It dangles from my fingers.
I coil saliva-damp orbs in my palm and offer them to the man

next to me. He yanks the strand apart and   white
       dots   scatter   across   asphalt.

I drop to the ground and gather rolling pearls. I scoop them
in my palms, but they slide through my fingers. They spiral

away from me, disappearing down sewers. I cough and more
spew out of my mouth, unstrung. I choke and blood oozes out

around the white balls. Each pearl is larger than the one before
and I know my throat will rupture. I cram one hand over

my mouth and press the other against my throat, try to press
the pearls back down my esophagus. They dribble out

and fall down, pooling around my legs. The asphalt turns
iridescent and the man shuffles away, kicking great clouds

of pearls. They fan up and he curses as they pelt his arms.
He flails his hands but still more shower down. His shoulders

hunch and he stumbles, the pearls roll his feet in circles. His body drops and still pearls boil from my mouth, shoot between

my fingers. His hand claws against the white tide but the orbs bury him and his fingertips drop below the pearl sea.

Adam's Revenge

You were livid,
weren't you
when God told
you Woman would
give birth—
blood burned under the
flesh of your cheeks,
your jaw clenched,
top molar crushed
into the bottom—
you became
the throwaway.
You never told her
about the Tree—
grinned as your teeth
tore flesh away
from the core.
God knew—
and tossed you out
with her.
You patted her
swollen belly,
felt those thumps
as your son kicked,
saw her eyes widen
with shock,
heard her breath

break with the first pain.
You wrapped your arms
around her, drew her into
your shelter,
told her God was like you—
male—
and she the throwaway.

Every Night is a Night of Bombs Somewhere

Most dances are cries. Try to pin them in place.
Look away from ash—a boy and a girl

loving that boy: screams and statues
flash-frozen against a night sky bleached white.

You and I are flesh. We slam together under a disco ball
moon that shreds the clouds. Our urgent legs reverb rhythm.

Light gilds your teeth. Another house shatters. The radio
                                            wobbles.
Chuck D. demands we *fight the power* and my hips swivel

a battle cry. As long as our feet pound
ground we're alive. The night shines. We explode.

We blink out the shine and darkness re-dawns.
The alarms die. Evening spreads: a patient bleeding on a table.

No ether. Dogs bark. I catch your mouth
with mine, eat vapor, and know tonight we die.

Thoughts while Smoking the Last Cigarette on the Porch in Summer

    I
Moths circle my roof
        diving into the emaciated
lamp light over the door.

    II
I dream cremation.
Flames shroud my ankles,
        slide along calves,
and lick my thighs.
Tongues flicker
        over my torso and
scorch my arms.
My fingers blaze
        and I trace letters in the smoke.

    III
In New Zealand, the dead
can return as moths.
A week or two
of lust for the moon
before dust.

Tell Stories if You Want the Adults to Listen

Jaws work up
         and down
                 the grown-ups' faces.
 The past drips out the corners
                     of their mouths and they wipe
         memory from their lips.
Plans for the future
        sparkle in their eyes
                swim out from behind teeth.
Nothing now.
Now is when I want.
        I want. I am waist
               high.
I want up. I want down.
        I want
               now. Now! NOW!

My howls wrap their past-future talk
               scream strands
twist around their sounds
               strangle their syllables
                  they pat me
                  talk
            about when I get older
                    how my baby days
             passed
             so quickly.

The Antler Woman Responds
After Mark Doty

On misty-gray, not-dark, not-light days
I feel bone sprout from my temples.
I try to catch a glimpse in store windows.

I should keep my eyes on the ground
instead of stepping out of forwardness.
But my allegiance is not to permanent forms.

Plain clothes hide hooves and haunches,
the elongated grammar of muscle,
and me without a trench coat.

I am the respiration of the grass
and my animal alphabet
fails on a regular basis.

Years from now on a tonal night
my feet will evaporate into cloud
and my antlers will twine with stardust.

For now I am less anatomy
than a storm, a glittering, gathering mass,
an antlered woman dodging traffic.

A Warning (Maybe)

I saw the
devil
leaning
on a white
picket fence
last night.

He tore the
petals off
a rose one
by one
and ate
the core.

Margaritas, Poolside

My glass sizzles with stars
or salt. Crystals slide down
and lime pricks my tongue.
We sit and watch children
splash in a pool. Not ours.
Just random apartment kids.

An average Southern summer
scene, but somehow this 90-degree
dusk differs from other
nights. Perhaps the extra
fifth of gold tequila
from the bargain rack

sliding through lime juice
makes the night unique.
Voices carry across water.
Pour another margarita
and watch sparkles bounce
against the glass's edge.

You stare at me. I
watch your bathing
neighbors. Your eyes
glow too much. Wet skin
at sunset allows my eyes
to rest and I swallow.

Half Light

I could say
we were together in
darkness but
it would be a lie.
The streetlight
shone in the window,
perhaps it was
the moon but it was so
yellow across the flesh
of your back and my fingers.
We shared a creaking
single bed, lying on our sides
I stared at the shadow
beneath your hair—outlined
by the almost light.
I know there were words—
I recall your voice
but only as touch—
your skin under my
fingers—
your palm slipping over
goosebumps I blamed on
the air conditioning.

It was not love.
Just two pieces
sliding together and to hell
with the rest of the box.

Frying Green Tomatoes

Pull the storm into your body.
Breathe the rain.

Brick walls hem us together.
My skin is too tight.

We count midnight eggs and crack
them against glass. Your fingers graze

mine as you take a bowl. Two greenish tomatoes glow
on the windowsill. My elbow catches a pot

and metal thunders against linoleum. The storm
slides across the sky and lightning blues the kitchen.

You toss a tomato through the flash and I snatch
the fruit. Green flesh oozes under the knife.

A jade sliver cools my fingers against your lips
and you bathe the medallions in egg.

Cornmeal coats them. Oil crackles.
Rain splatters on the window and slices

drop from your palms. Golden circles
float in oil. Wind flings water against glass.

You fish tomatoes from oil. They drain
on towels and we wait.

Infatuectomy

wind slices
my skin
a scalpel
opening me
to remove
the parasite
that slid
into my ear
when you said
my name

In the Dark

The cacophony of color
drains from the drapes
and soaks the rug.
Near the hamper
your red shirt bleeds
into my purple skirt.

All fades to gray
or to nothing, if the night
is dark enough.

I understand refraction
and reflection
but it shocks
me each night
when color exists
then doesn't exist
then does again
with the flick
of a switch.

Midnight Scenes

                      The ceiling fan dips to kiss me.
I melt into my mattress and the springs close
        over my head.

              *

My lover sleeps and no fan sways low. I pull his hand
            into mine. His fingers drop into my palm.
I swallow them, one by one, ten long pills
                     no water to flood
them down my throat.

             **

Aurora borealis smears the Missouri sky. I go inside Christmas,
            the house where my grandfather died.
He carves a turkey. I tell him the dead do not carve the dead.
He tells me I am naive.

             ***

                  The toilet perches 12 feet above the floor
I cast a grappling hook into the bowl, twist up the rope.
A cave gapes in the wall.
        I crawl over the tank, into the cave
            where a crone feeds bones to a fire.
I yank my tibia free.
It ignites.

Why I Smoke in the Morning

My jaws clench and my molars jam
against each other until my face aches.
I'm not angry
I'm not in danger.
I'm too close to myself—
I hold my parts too tightly.

After the fire sinks to ash
and the smoke dwindles
to a slip of incense in a corner
the world slides apart just enough
for me to open my mouth.

Reading Fitzgerald in June
*Female Photuris fireflies mimic the mating flashes
of other fireflies for the purpose of predation.*

Gatsby believed in the green
light. No docks, no water
behind my house. Only
a patch of grass gray

with evening. A million
yellow lights pinhole the navy
shroud. Echoes glow from bladed
bowers. A man-firefly slips

down through grass and into
                the woman's mouth.

In *el Mercado*

Spanish syllables drift along *la avenida*[1]
and lick the salt from our margaritas.

Guitar riffs prickle *la brisa*[2]
and sink into *nuestro pozole.*[3]

We stir notes *con cuchares*[4]
and lift them a *las bocas.*[5]

---

[1] The avenue.
[2] The breeze.
[3] Our pozole—a hominy and pork stew that is believe to have Aztec origins.
[4] With spoons.
[5] To our mouths.

Dear Prufrock

It's never been a question
to eat the peach or not.

Measure my days
in cola cans and cigarette butts.

When the mermaids sing
I plug my ears. I am not Odysseus.

The women here do not
 remember Michelangelo.

The evening shrinks from sleep,
breathes heavily and lurks.

The universe is already disturbed.
I need not add to it.

A minute's decisions and revisions
will wind the world to the right again.

Unroll the bottoms of your trousers.
Drag them through the wake.

First Communion

Sunday after high Mass I skinned my knee the first
time I rode a bike. Friday evening now: I'm not sure why your
                                                    tongue
slipping syllables around my neck and tracing circles on my
                                                    throat
reminds me of church bells, flying over handlebars, torn skin,
crushed grass, and clouds framed by spinning tires.
You cup my breast and your breath covers my body.

I float above us; watch you animate my body.
Your fingers sketch Sanskrit up my spine: the first
union spelled across my back. Your hand tires.
Your lips part and words trip from your tongue.
My ears are submerged, drowning. Electricity jolts my skin
particles mambo over my shoulders and slide down my throat;

light nuclei shoved together over sheets. Energy escapes my
                                                    throat,
drenches the mattress, scorches the headboard. We are one body
writhing and fusing, there is no seam between your hand and my
                                                    skin.
This is church, this is resurrection, our ceremony granting the
                                                    first
benediction. The prayer that I trace on your neck with my
                                                    tongue
shakes psalms from your pores. You are David before he tires.

A chariot passes the bedpost, wooden wheels become tires.
The horse snorts; exhaust escapes his throat
in a violent gust. It is time to climb aboard while the chariot's
                              tongue
swings low. We thrash to the edge of the groaning mattress, our
                              body
a tangled a knot of flesh. We're stuck: too many hands, first,
then too few feet. We can't leave this wreckage of us, our
                              sanctuary of skin.

My voice speaks with your mouth. Your words wear my
                              syllables. My skin
covers your ribs. Scars web us together; your injuries fuse to
                              mine. Our body tires;
numbness washes over our brow and drips down a leg first,
then trickles between lips and crawls over a tongue to the throat.
Our eyelids shudder, they crash down and the body
fissions along the curves. Last the tongue

divides, housed once more in two caves. My lips freeze over my
                              tongue;
perhaps it's yours. I'm not sure what parts went into which skin
and I know the fingers attached feel heavier than the ones my
                              body
started with. Light filters over your chest, my wrist tires
from the weight of these new fingers. I hear syllables swim in
                              your throat,
my ears surface and your words sweep along the tide: *you were
                              first.*

My tongue struggles, tangled in my lips. You were first;
I can't wash you from my skin. The words tickle my throat,
my body wants to fly through clouds and spinning tires.

Cutting the Cake

When I cut my double she bled pink
                              because that's what we filled her
with.

I pressed a hunk of her against my groom's lips.
                                        His tongue slipped
between those lips,
                      and licked her sweet
                                  cream from my fingers.

The knife parted her layers
                          like clouds. She resisted less
              than I,
and I resisted less than grass resists wind.

We fed her to our guests.
                      They circled the table, sniffing.
          My aunt
                      took the knife from my fingers

sliced my twin neatly, one hunk per plate.
                                  She licked pink
                        from the blade.

In the Studio, After
(for E. S.)

A single moth flaps
                against the window.

Indigo-caked paintbrushes perch
                on the easel.

Frayed rope fibers scatter
                on the floor.

Your shadow sways
                over the canvas.

       ∞

Indigo-caked paintbrushes scatter
                on the floor.

A single moth sways
                over the canvas.

Your shadow flaps
                against the window.

Frayed rope fibers perch
                on the easel.

      ∞

Your shadow scatters
                on the floor.

Indigo-caked paintbrushes flap
                against the window.

Frayed rope fibers sway
                over the canvas.

A single moth perches
                on the easel.

No Bukowski

Staring into the abyss
or maybe it's the toilet
after a handful of pills
and a fifth of whiskey,
not Jack Daniels, but
something in a plastic
bottle from the bottom
shelf. Either way, it's
dark and the surface
ripples. An eye winks,
or perhaps it's the flush-
ing water's swirl.

The plan never includes
knees freezing on cold
tile. No mention of vomit
and a bloody throat
when the party starts.
But it ends the same.
Philosophical rambling
to the crapper between
heaves. No romance
and it hurts the writer in me.
I'm no Bukowski.

Nataraja on Broadway

I.

       Siva dances.
Flames devour
                the jagged fingers
                          of the city skyline.
His feet smash
      the ground
and tornados swirl
        off his arms.

            Wall Street's crumbs
                   flour the street.

His hair snakes out,
                  catches his children.
          They bathe in the river
                gushing down his face.

II.

Siva dances.
                His feet rhythm
through concrete.
                Orange blooms
spring out of rubble.

Hitchhikers

Voices spin   round the tires
           trucks speed past the men
carrying their lives in backpacks.

A limp thumb pops out
           of one man's pocket
and flutters at the traffic.

      No one stops.
           the other two men shrug and amble
           on down the median, slouching to dawn.

My Daughter's Monologue

I let my brother go
first—he kept push-
push-pushing my spine.
I stepped aside and he tip-
ped over the edge.

You promised to open
again four years later.

My brother turns 9 and I still
wait for the opening.

Sorrow does not open wombs.
He stole my place and you—
you embrace him. Your arms
wrap around his stolen body.

My body. His now. He spits out
where I meant to open.
He spits forth, I wanted to hold.
I wanted a tunnel
he filled with a beam.

Healing

After Encephalitis

The mosquito sucked the maps
out of your mind
with a serrated needle
and left your brain
to swell against your skull.

18 wheels spun to a stop
and you called for directions
two blocks from work,
18 years on the job.

The receptionist didn't recognize
your voice. She asked you to repeat
your name three times.
Ed? This can't be Ed.
Is this a joke?

You assured her this was no gag.
I can't rightly remember
if I turn left or right
and has the Sphinx
at the corner of 5th
and Main always been there?

She talked you through
the right turn and stoplight.
Aren't you the guy
who drives through L.A.
without a map?
You tried to laugh.
Drove. I drove through L.A.

You left the truck in the lot,
when you arrived two hours later,
got into your Studebaker,
and drove into the desert
coasting along the blind road.

Eric, after the Throat Slashing

One foot
    forward,
drag-shuffle the other
                I heard the voice before
                I saw her in the gas pump's shadow.
                She said, s*ome dudes, they jumped me.*

Fingers pinch skin shut.
    Stumble against the curb.
Blood coppers the wedding band.
                She was so small, her eyes wet
                      and wide. Her lips soft around
              words, *I'm not from around here.*

Snapshots of my wife,
        my daughter
    blur past irises.
                Already late, Friday. I told my
                wife I'd be back by ten.
The girl only
        needed a sec,
            Can I just use your phone real quick?
One foot
    forward,
drag-shuffle the other.

          It was cold. Her fingers slid
          around my phone, numb.
                Aw shit, man, I dropped your
                phone. Where'd it go?

Lean against a florist's
        door, jangle the hanging
strap of bells.

                I knelt and reached; she sank
            down on my back,
                her hand dragged metal over my
            throat. Those soft lips snarled,
                Where do you think you're going?

Lean against the wall,
        force eyes open and watch
red and blue bloom closer and closer.

Faulkner's Rebellious Woman

I am the dirt poor female in a novel Faulkner never finished.
Perhaps I assume too many pages for myself. Maybe I'm
a short story. Last night the boy—we're not sure if he's bad or
                                                                        mixed

up—exploded my house with me and my family inside.
I didn't much care for the family. They're very Faulkner:
Father limps and slaps without feeling. Mother fades

into the wall and sighs. I did not blow up. I climbed
out the window. I am not supposed to climb, but I do.
My feet hit the turf and I run, run, run. The boy sees me

and chases. I am the running Faulkner heroine. I do not walk.
No tragedy swells my belly. He pitches my pages into the fire
but I float away. I am not ash.

Seasonal Sleep

Sleep leaves my room
each spring, lured out the door
by honeysuckle and birdsong.

I spend the nights in books
or spread paint and call forth
new companions in canvas.

Not until the midsummer heat
melts me to my sheets
will sleep slide back into bed.

Rainy Supper

The rain continues. Water
splatters the windows, drills
into the roof. Gray light all
day. Everyday. Gray fades
to black and it is night.

We crouch in the den. Curled
under a blanket, my son and I.
He leans against my shoulder
and asks for food. I heat a pan
on the hotplate next to us,

drop in a hunk of meat, stir.
The sizzle fills the room
and drowns the rain. I scoop
the meat out of the pan, feed
it to my son and notice a gash

the same shape on my palm.
The wound is dry, no blood,
just hollow beneath the thumb.
My son eats and I ask if he wants
more as I take his hand.

A Dozen Small Perceptions before Dusk

The dwindling light slips through the dusky leaves
of the magnolia tree with the wilting pink blooms.
The light barely slides over the steps of the porch.
My feet rest on wood inches from the border of light,
gently they press against the slats and sway my body on
the glider. The bulb above me remains dark.

Moths beat wings against the spreading dark,
beg for the bulb to be lit. Wind rustles flowers and leaves.
The sparrow's nest sways; one chirp slips out. Light only on
the edge of the steps. I watch shadows bloom,
deaf to the pleas of moths. I refuse to let it be light.
My seat slides beneath me, stretches my legs over the porch.

My feet skid over the wood. A breeze tiptoes up the porch
steps and brushes my ankles. The moths rebuff my dark
sanctuary from glaring streetlights.
The cat twines my legs, pats my leg with a paw, then leaves:
a gray tail waves above the bush. Another cat voice blooms
over the cricket chirps and rustling grass. A dog barks in the
                          yard on

my left, the grate reminds me of starting a car on
a snowy morning. An incongruent image now on the porch.
I wait for the warmth to drift away into the night, to kiss blooms
of magnolia goodnight, to let the cool night air settle, a dark

blanket punctuated by star buttons. It is too early, the day still
                              leaves
saying prolonged goodbyes. A day reluctant to end, creeping
                              light

dragging its feet off of the stairs. Now it lingers on the walk,
                              light
feet barely touch the ground. The crickets change tune on
a cue from the wind. The laziness of the hot day leaves.
Chaotic night ushers in staccato beat from the chorus beneath
                              the porch.
The scent of rain trickles into the air; a scent both light and dark:
the smell of melon edged in mud like the blooms

of the tree in front—pale pink centers surrounded by magenta
                              blooms
to gown a pixie. Pinpoints of yellow dot the lawn. Light
is a shield against loneliness; visible voices shout against the
                              dark.
A creak from a door spring and my husband steps on
the smooth wood and finds me in the shadows of the porch:
our suburban watchtower. He brushes fallen leaves

from a seat. They whisper fall. We bloom now: leaves
unfurled by the summer's last light on the edge of the porch.
The dark blankets us as we breathe, gliding on and on.

Labyrinth

      *

The mermaid swimming
         between mossy roots
in my backyard looks
         me in the eye and winks.
I yank the curtains off
         the rod and shatter the bedroom window.
Leviathan whisper-shouts my name.
         Syllables drip off
the tongue, slide
         past teeth wrapping
around my neck.
         I dive down his spiral coils
and swim.
         Twisted scales undulate
around a temple wall.
         I slip through a gap
and tumble into a window.

      *

Clerics chase me
         down the mildewing hall.
I clutch dirty dishes
         under my robe.

A sharp turn
  and a splintered wall
disrobes me.
    Silverware clatters.
I crawl down
  the hallway
the rough carpet
  scrapes my knees.

 *

I stand in the garden
  and brush parsley off
my skin. Between my fingers
    thyme crumbles and blows
out of my hand. I smell my palms
  embrace the gray scent.

Breakfast, Too Early, on the Patio in June

A 12-inch stallion
grazes in Virginia Creeper
surrounding the patio.

A squirrel squawks,
the stallion's head jerks
from the green.

His nose tests the air,
muscles undulate under
charcoal fur. He bolts.

I step to the Virginia Creeper
and gaze at the patch,
tooth marks scallop the leaves.

An empty statue base
with four hoof prints
sinks into the mud.

Evening Bread
for Rook

You slipped into the cove between
your father and me when the moon
stole down from the sky. You swam
a sea of navy blue quilts, and sailed
over the rim of chenille.
Now the sunlight is eleven
and slides around the drape's edge.

We should be up—
we should have been up hours ago:
me in the kitchen frying eggs
while you watch puppets recite the alphabet.
Instead, your head brushes my neck,
tucks under my chin to sleep.
My arms anchor you to me.
Tonight you will pull your chair
to the counter: we will bake evening bread.

Massaged by Hooves

Two equine women pummeled my body, air snorting from their long noses as they kneaded the dough of my back. Their hooves clopped softly against the plush carpet. They pulled my arms and tugged my shoulders into alignment. My muscles moaned and their ears swiveled away from the glowing music box. A studio storm thundered, drizzled through speakers. The rain rinsed the rush hour traffic-horn-honking-squealing-breaks from my ears. The women whinnied at me and rubbed apple oil on my temples. They covered my eyes and shined a thousand watt lamp over my face, nickered over my pores, neighed about deep cleansing treatments and the dangers of hot showers and cold wind. They whickered and my neck melted against their palms. I dropped the weight of my head.

Gaea's Saturday Morning
to Prufrock

Shall I press
the blue snooze button?
Let the planets sleep
while the stars dream?

Watch them roll over,
listen to them murmur
while I scrub the meteor shower,
tighten the asteroid belts,
rinse and polish the supernova,
smooth the solar flares
and fold the cosmos.

Even in my sleep,
my feet hurt.
The astral kitchen
light glares off
the celestial stove
when I cook.

I, too, have storms.

Ingesting the Storm

Rain blazes down my skin,
                                      burns paths between freckles.
                      Lightning tears my hair.
       I tilt my head back
and water chars
            my throat.

Baby Book

I never filled your baby book.
<u>   </u>
<u>   </u>

I opened it in hushed moments
<u>   </u>
<u>   </u>

while you slept in intensive care.
<u>   </u>
<u>   </u>

                        I peered at you through plastic walls,
                        my hand in your aquarium-cage.
                        My first blanket was <u>green, maybe</u>?

                        My first ventilator tube was <u>blue,</u>
                        <u>*dark blue down your throat.*</u>

A pouch for your first fingernail. [_]

A page for your sonogram.

          Nothing for
the first x-ray—the unripe lungs.

One for the first picture.
Empty. (   ).

Business Lunch

A squirrel pitched an acorn
that bounced off my head.
He scolded from his oak fortress.

I invaded his leafy patio.
I explained that my
path was random.

He tilted his head.
I didn't hear fury
when he chittered.

Another acorn dropped.
I caught it and cracked the shell.
He nodded and broke open a twin.

The golden flesh was bitter
eaten raw like that.
But with company, bearable.

Revelation

Industrial Revelation

God fogs out.
I see the dirt
swirl behind him.
Dust devils cyclone
in hell's shadow,
flooding the earth with sand.
A man drowns
in the mirage.
Day falls. Night blazes
Our daily drought
gags us.
Rain evaporates 30 feet
above the ground.

Treading Water with Uncle Bill

A bullet bored through Uncle Bill's
head one night after a bottle of whiskey
barreled down his throat.

Uncle Bill tore down tenements
and dragged slum lords to the poor
house. In the ghetto I heard his name

pronounced like a saint's and up at the country
 club they cursed it as soon as he left the room.
Twice I dreamt about him. Once, the night

before he died: he sits in my mother's
kitchen and we chat. At the end he stares
at me until I look away. The next afternoon

my mother called and informed me.
The second, a year later: we meet
at a pool—not the country club pool

where he soaked with the soakers—
but the bug filled blue hole outside
a South Louisiana apartment.

We dive in and tread water, wasp
corpses float and roaches drift toward
 us. The water rises. Our legs bicycle

and arms helicopter to keep
our heads above water.
I try to swim to the ladder but waves

knock me back to the center where
Bill calmly bobs. *You can't get
out. Stay and talk.* My legs churn.

Water creeps up my neck,
floods over my chin.

Urban Primitive

I wrap the bundle of my brain
in a leaf plucked from the snow
caught in the urban undertow.
My stilettos smack the pavement.

    Recuerda, las uñas de la zorra son cuchillos.[6]

Abuela[7] warns you about me.
I wander past *la iglesia en la mañana*[8].
A gray curl slips out of the black lace.
Her words tug your ear, pull your eyes off me.

    Ella anda en el miasma de la ciudad.[9]

I sling the bundle around a stick,
and toss it over my shoulder while
hiking down *el camino.*[10]
Leather rides up my hips.

    Ojos incandescentes en la sombra.[11]

---

[6] Remember, the claws of the vixen are knives
[7] Grandmother.
[8] The church in the morning.
[9] She walks in the miasma of the city.
[10] The road
[11] Incandescent eyes in the shadow.

Easier to walk the city with my brain
a neat parcel on my shoulder,
bouncing in time to my steps.
My breasts shimmer in a silver halter.

        Ella come la tierra.[12]

---

[12] She eats the earth.

Swamp Swim

     Swan against the waves
                 and frog in the wake.
     We lie on lily pads
and you skim the water
                 with your toes.
     My fingers flick dew drops
from your lips and we roll
                 off the lily
     and under algae.

Bath

after Langston Hughes

The calm,
Cool face of the river
Asked me for a kiss

and it sucks the air
out of my lungs
replaces it with acid
eyes shut tight
like you told me
they should be when you kissed my
nine-year-old lips
with your forty-year-old ones.
my lungs
burn with water

your hand print rinses off.

Lactation Lament

Nine months into my daughter's
life, I am crawling
myself to bed each night
and dreaming of freedom
from her mouth.

I lack the skills or patience
for proper lactation
yet the Jewish-Catholic guilt
of my childhood commands
I let my daughter draw

strength from my body.
Perhaps it is the sitting
for minute stacked on hour,
becoming one with cushions,
submerging into the sofa.

Or perhaps it is the scent
of milk everywhere. In shirts,
bras, and even waistbands. Shields
do not defend against smells,
and I hate the odor of milk.

Dead Mermaids

I meet Turtle Head Woman at the university café. The day is swampy and she revels in the damp ooze mudding the sidewalk cracks. Obviously she is a café regular; no one stares at her bald greengray head or pointed lipless mouth. She smiles a poet's smile and nudges me away from my pen with dry claws. *It's not a matter of talent*, she informs me. *Poetry's dead*. She dribbles tea in a saucer and laps the amber liquid with her graveled tongue. She closes her eyes and raises her snout to sniff the summer air. When her eyelids crack open she grumbles, *You're still here. Don't you get it? The mermaids won't sing to you.*

Shake the Dust from My Tongue

Waking after death isn't the difficulty.
The eyelids open. It takes a moment
to properly focus. But often there's not

much to see, as coffins allow little light.
The casket presents the greatest challenge.
I prefer wood because it crumbles,

and I can hurry it along with my claws.
Grave dirt parts before my fingers—my own Red
Sea and my tribe of one climbs to grass.

Aluminum irritates me and I have to hope
for a hurricane to wash me down Bourbon Street
or a grave robber to crack my lid.

Once the lid's gone, it's a simple matter
of stretching, a few sharp cracks of the neck,
and I shake the dust from my tongue.

A Defeated Caffeine Junky Remembers the War

I named myself
General and commanded
my kidneys: accept less
water; more caffeine.

Two months of messages
I censored.
They mutinied,
spilled first
blood: Red seared
from my urethra
and splattered
against white porcelain.

Single combat
settled the conflict.
They sent their hero:
the bladder. It spasmed.
I crumpled against
the tile field. I waved a white
cloth and swore obedience
to my body.
I pay tribute:
glass-after-glass of water.

Scout

On horseback he cuts
the road in half
with his shadow

stretching over corpses
who do not yet know
they are dead.

Dust swirls behind,
drifts over hands
reaching for the stirrups.

A coyote calls. No
answer. Another town
waits around the bend.

Insomnia Rag, Minor Key

Insomnia crawls over the carpet,
creeps along my leg, slides into my ears,
exits my mouth, and plays on the radio.
The guitar riffs: my audible lack of sleep.

I murmur *Shantih, shantih, shantih* to a cat,
stare at a flickering screen, press my face
into a pillow, force my eyes to close. The night
light in the bathroom presses against my skin.

The curve of his neck disintegrates. I am a stranger
to my sheets. The blanket does not know my name.

Discussing the Romantics

Turtle Head Woman snaps her beak
                    and wags her stumpy head.
Her glossy eyes
                roll in their sockets.
She wraps her arms
                    around her chest
—which is human—
              and rocks
back
            and
forth in her seat.

No shell
        just soft, sagging
skin wrapping her bones.

Her neck accordions,
              then collapses her chin
to her collar.

She mumbles about Keats, Shelley, and Byron
      before the wool
               turtleneck swallows her head.

Storyless

I remained without history, living in the woods where wolves ask few questions. They come to tea and recite verses in moonlight, but questions rarely leave their tongues. On afternoons when the sun hangs low and dribbles between the trees, an ear might cock to the side and an inquiry might begin. A shrug and a scone pushed across the table with cream shoves the curiosity aside. They are not like cats. Cats ask and ask. Cats do not distract so easily. I swallow my stories with honey and lemon.

Buddy at the Casino

The first time my dead dog
spoke, I sat in a casino
in front of a double star penny slot.
A cigarette burned
against my writing callous.
The smoke outlined his pointed
ears and enough of his wispy
beard that I knew the Yorkie face.
He said, *press the max bet button,*
and so I bet ninety cents.
Too many pennies
to bet on one whirl of fruit
and sevens. But he spoke
with a terrier's confidence,
and I wanted to feel
that energy again. Sure enough,
no jackpot, but a ten-
dollar win. No sirens, no casino
attendant. Just a lot of clanking,
a melting daiquiri,
and a dog ghost
threaded in Camel smoke.

A Retired Miner Describes Work

This is what it looks like when you walk into the earth:
the black swallows your body.
The sun is memory.
The dark is better
than light. You see
everything: color is sharp
and precise,
not dull and fuzzy
like on the surface.
The details carved in stone
knobs glint and reflect quartz.
Crystals form waterfalls
on every side.
Pathways glow beneath your feet
and stars line the walls.

To walk in the earth is easy.
It does not move through
you. You move through rocks,
pebbles, fine dirt as if air, but so very rich:
Your bones and muscles renew.
You are young and at your peak.
Sound is not there, but you hear from within
like seeing in heavy fog.
When a pixie laughs you feel the joy inside.
Sound waves are unnecessary
inside a mother cradling her child
in the sweet and savory taste of love.

Bedroom Mutation

Snapping boards keep me awake
nights. A deep sound where

my room's walls pull out
of the foundation, and tonight

I hear carpet rip away
from the door.

Drainpipe arms sprout
from the window

and scrape their nails
against glass.

Chunks of first floor wall
support my room

as it leaps to the grass
and strides west.

About the Author

Ki Russell teaches writing, literature, and creative writing at Blue Mountain Community College in Pendleton, Oregon, where she resides with her husband Timothy and two children, Rook and Ashe. She also serves a cat Draco and a new border collie-blue heeler mix, Dooby Dooby Doo.

This year, Ars Omnia will publish her experimental novel, *The Wolf at the Door*, a modern fairy tale containing poetry. Medulla Publishing released her chapbook, *How to Become Baba Yaga* in 2011.

Ki researches fairy tales, then butchers them for her own purposes. She steals time from grading to wrestle with words, converse with the cat, dance with the dog, and paint.

She holds a Ph.D. in English literature (Creative Writing emphasis) from the University of Louisiana at Lafayette and an M.A. in English (Creative Writing emphasis) from the University of Missouri-Kansas City.

She believes people should laugh more.

Books by Paladin Contemporaries:

Cicada Grove (1992). A novella by Lindsey Martin-Bowen. A few copies available by mail order only. ISBN 1-881048-01-2

THE DOWRY OF DONNA BEACH. Songs for a Woman's Voice. (1999). Compiled by Pat Huyett, who composed some of the lyrics. (Arvada House Press, a poetry division of Paladin Contemporaries). Out-of-print. ISBN 1-881048-03-9.

El Dorado Rosa: Voices from Midtown. (1999) Poetry chapbook by Pat Huyett. (Arvada House Press, a poetry division of Paladin Contemporaries). Out-of-Print. ISBN 1-881048-04-7.

*Grand Unified Theory: The Unauthorized Fragment*s. (2001), Poetry by Robert E. Haynes. ISBN 1-881048-02-0.
13-digit ISBN 978-1-881048-

Hamburger Haven. (2009). A novel by Lindsey Martin-Bowen. ISBN 1-881048-05-5. 13-digit ISBN 978-1-881048-05-3.

Rapture Redux: *A Novel.* (2014). By Lindsey Martin-Bowen. ISBN 1-881048-08-X. 13-digit ISBN 978-1-881048-08-4.

Antler Woman Responds. (2014) Poetry by Ki Russell. ISBN 1-881048-07-1. 13-digit ISBN 978-1-881048-07-7.

Love one another. John 13:34.

www.ingramcontent.com/pod-product-compliance
Lightning Source LLC
LaVergne TN
LVHW041633070426
835507LV00008B/599